Can the Devil Read My Mind?

DAVID CASSIDY

C·C

Can the Devil Read My Mind?
By David Cassidy

© 2021 Core Christianity
13230 Evening Creek Drive
Suite 220-222
San Diego, CA 92128

Design and Creative Direction by Metaleap Creative

Printed in the United States of America

First Printing—October 2021

CONTENTS

"And [Jesus] said to them, 'I watched Satan fall from heaven like lightning.'"

Luke 10:18

The Prince of Darkness Grim

THE FIRST TIME I EVER thought seriously about Satan was while singing a hymn. At the Lutheran church I grew up in, we sang Protestant Reformer Martin Luther's "A Mighty Fortress" with passion and resilient faith. While extolling God's power to protect and save his people, Luther's lyrics also note the presence of Satan and his hatred of all who follow Christ. I'll never forget the effect of these lines:

> For still our ancient foe
> doth seek to work us woe;
> his craft and power are great,
> and armed with cruel hate,
> on earth is not his equal. . . .
> The prince of darkness grim,
> we tremble not for him;
> his rage we can endure,
> for lo! his doom is sure;
> one little word shall fell him.

Luther, a man with a price on his head, was keenly aware of Satan's opposition. As he worked to reform the church, he saw Satan's lies and the power of false accusations inspired by his malevolent intent. Despite all these threats from the "Prince of Darkness grim," the Reformer didn't tremble. Neither should we. We have to be aware of Satan, but at the same time, we confess and live in the transforming grace of Jesus' victory over him on our behalf.

Luther took his cues from Scripture, of course—especially the apostles. He could no doubt sense the ominous footfall of the one Peter described as a "your adversary" who "prowls around like a roaring lion, seeking someone to devour" (1 Pet. 5:8).[1] Yet he also believed that Jesus "appeared ... to destroy the works of the devil" (1 John 3:8) and that God would "soon crush" this terrible foe "under your feet" (Rom. 16:20). Paul told the fledgling congregations in Asia Minor that they were in the fight of their lives, a struggle for their souls and for the progress of the gospel in the world. The battle was "not against flesh and blood, but against the rulers, against the powers, against the world forces of this darkness, against the spiritual forces of wickedness in the heavenly places" (Eph. 6:12). For such a fight they would need to "take up the full armor of God" (Eph. 6:13).

The Christian's life is a battle. The sooner we come to terms with the rage of our enemy and learn to depend on the power of the Lord of Hosts for our strength in the conflict, the sooner we'll be able to properly equip ourselves. Like all soldiers, we need solid intel on our foe, including familiarity with his tactics and weapons. We also need to know our own weapons and how to deploy them. Paul wrote to Timothy that he should be prepared to "suffer hardship with me, as a good soldier of Jesus Christ" (2 Tim. 2:3). This isn't an easy battle, and it will last our entire lives. If we understand the nature of this warfare, the enemy we face, and how God has acted in Christ to deliver us from evil and defeat the powers of Satan, then at the end we'll be able to say with Paul, "I fought the good fight . . . I have kept the faith" (2 Tim. 4:7).

That's why this subject is important. As Christians we want to see Jesus' victory over the darkness extended into the whole world. We desire to please God, not giving into the subtle and sometimes violent ways Satan

---

1   Unless otherwise marked, all Scripture quotations are taken from the *The New American Bible* (United States: St. Anthony Guild Press, 1970).

seeks to overthrow our faith. We also want to discern Satan's footprints as he seeks to trap our friends and family with his lies, stealing from them life and joy in the gospel.

The wonderful British author C.S. Lewis wrote, "There are two equal and opposite errors into which our race can fall about the devils. One is to disbelieve in their existence. The other is to believe, and to feel an excessive and unhealthy interest in them. They themselves are equally pleased by both errors and hail a materialist[2] or a magician with the same delight."[3]

In this booklet, we'll look to avoid those twin errors and instead grasp two great truths. The first is that we really do have a sinister enemy. He's the devil, or Satan, and he's joined by a great many lesser creatures called demons in his efforts to despoil God's world, destroy God's people, and deny Christ's gospel. The second is that we really do have a mighty savior, the Lord Jesus Christ, the incarnate Lord of Mighty Angels, who has come to deliver everyone bound by the devil, disarm the darkness through his cross, and destroy this enemy forever.

Jesus and Satan are not equals battling for an uncertain outcome. Our Savior has already conquered this foe through his death and resurrection, crushing Satan's head beneath his nail-scarred heel and extending the boundaries of his kingdom through the gospel. Knowing that this is the case, let's now turn to what the Scriptures say about Satan. Laying aside the popular images we may have in our heads, we'll learn where he came from, what he's capable of, and what will become of him.

---

2   By *materialist*, Lewis isn't referring to a greedy person but to someone who believes that reality consists only in what can be known by our senses and denies the reality of an unseen world.

3   C.S. Lewis, *The Screwtape Letters* (New York: HarperOne, 2009), ix.

"Your adversary, the devil, prowls around like a roaring lion, seeking someone to devour."

1 Peter 5:8

CHAPTER ONE

Your Adversary the Devil

THE CANDY BOWL IS READY by the door. The witch's caldron on the porch steams, with party-store eyes floating in a brew of green slime. The doorbell rings and on your doorstep await the cutest collection of kiddos: fairies, movie stars, superheroes, and the most darling devil you've ever seen. "Trick or Treat!" they all scream, their tiny hands grabbing a candy bar or three.

This annual rite of Halloween brings laughter and cavities to many people. But have you ever wondered if our view of Satan might be shaped more by that little devil at the door than by Scripture? When you stop to think about it, do you really know who—or what—the devil is and what he's trying to do? Is Satan for real? Is he everywhere, all-knowing, and all-powerful—a kind of mirror image of God, but bad instead of good? Are God and Satan two equals battling it out for cosmic supremacy? Why does God allow Satan to do anything at all?

Good questions. Let's dig in.

THE DEVIL IMAGINED

The name *Satan* has its origin in the Hebrew word *ha-satan*, and it means *the adversary*. The name *devil* has a Greek origin, *diabolos*, from which we get our word *diabolical*. It means *divider, slanderer,* or *accuser*.

Both are present in this exhortation to the church from the apostle Peter: "Be sober-minded; be watchful. Your adversary the devil prowls around like a roaring lion, seeking someone to devour" (1 Pet. 5:8 ESV[1]). Peter was well aware of this ancient foe's attempts to confuse, deceive, possess, slander, murder, enslave, tempt, and oppress people. If he took Satan's opposition to the church seriously, warning us to be "on the alert" against him, we'd best take the adversary seriously as well.

To do this, we need to develop our views on the devil and dark powers from the Bible, and that starts with clearing away misconceptions about him. It's probably safe to say that most people's images of the devil are informed more by pop culture and literature than by Scripture. There's a long and colorful history of portraying the devil in both Near-Eastern and Western art. Some of the earliest visual depictions of the devil show him as a version of *Pan*, the half-human, half-goat Greco-Roman fertility god. This is where depictions of the devil with hoofs and horns originate. Norse and other European gods had similar forms and were known to rule over the realm of the dead, known as hel. The red-suited, pitch-fork toting devil who rules over hell and is depicted in cartoons and Halloween costumes owes more to mythology than the Bible.

Dante's *Inferno* shows the devil as a three-faced monster with six giant bat wings. He's frozen in ice in the deepest part of hell, imprisoned there forever, gnawing on the head of Judas Iscariot. In *Paradise Lost*, John Milton portrays the devil as Lucifer, ruling in Hell's capital city of Pandemonium with the help of lesser fallen angels who've been thrown out of heaven along with him. He responds to his exile with the famous line, "It is better to reign in hell than serve in heaven." Milton makes Satan a complex, subtle, almost sympathetic figure. He notes that Satan's fall

---

1 Scripture quotations labeled "ESV" are from the *ESV® Bible* (*The Holy Bible, English Standard Version®*), Copyright © 2001 by Crossway, a publishing ministry of Good News Publishers. Used by permission. All rights reserved.

was due to pride, while his tactics to bring about the fall of Adam and Eve were rooted in calculated deception.

Milton's Satan is clever and keenly aware of the weaknesses in his human targets. In Goethe's *Faust*, the devil wants to lead Faust astray by getting him to sell his soul in exchange for unlimited knowledge and pleasure. More recently, in *Memnoch the Devil*, Anne Rice portrays Satan as attractive, cool, smart, and desirable. Who could possibly say 'No' to such a beautiful being?

To this day, these sinister, powerful, seductive, and intelligent images of our adversary show up in films like Disney's *Fantasia* and songs like *The Devil Went Down to Georgia*. While great poems, songs, and films should be enjoyed, we must also realize that these mythological images of Satan often leave a mark on our minds. They can make his character loom larger in our thoughts than is appropriate, leading us to believe he's more intelligent and powerful than he actually is. On the other hand, we may consider him ridiculous and therefore easily dismissed. Looking to Scripture will help us avoid these extremes, enabling us to discard unhelpful myths while taking the biblical warnings seriously.

WHERE DID THE DEVIL COME FROM?

On many Sunday mornings, the church I grew up in used the Nicene Creed to confess our faith. Summarizing what the church believes about the Father, the Son, the Spirit, the church, and the final judgment at Christ's return, it begins, "I believe in one God, the Father Almighty, maker of heaven and earth, and of all things visible and *invisible*" (italics mine).[2] God is the Creator not only of all that we can see but also of

---

2   Burn, A. E. 1909. The Nicene creed (London: Rivingtons).

all that's hidden from our eyes. In addition to the world we enjoy and explore through our senses, there's a dimension to the creation that isn't seen by us even though we experience its influence. This is the realm of the angels.

"How did God create angels?" the Westminster Larger Catechism asks. It answers, "God created all the angels as spirits, immortal, holy, excelling in knowledge, mighty in power, to execute his commandments, and to praise his name, yet subject to change."[3] We hold that God made everything good. This includes all the angels, who are referred to in Scripture as holy (see Ps. 89:5–7). This invisible realm predates the visible creation. Job 38:7 records God saying, "When the stars were made, all my angels praised me with a loud voice." What a magnificent choir that was!

In the Bible, angels serve God by serving as mediators of his message, carrying out his will in the world, inspiring human action, inflicting his judgments, and delivering his people from danger. They are "ministering spirits, sent out to provide service for the sake of those who will inherit salvation" (Heb. 1:14). For example, the angel Gabriel tells Mary she will be Jesus' mother and exhorts Joseph to take her as his wife. Another angel announces Jesus' birth to the shepherds on a Bethlehem hillside (Luke 1:26–38; Matt. 1:18–21). Angels minister to Jesus after Satan tempts him (Matt. 4; Luke 4), and Jesus tells his disciples that he can ask the Father for "twelve legions of angels" to rescue him from the cross if he wants to do so (Matt. 26:53). That's 72,000 angels! When one considers that a *single angel* once killed an entire Assyrian army of 185,000 soldiers (Isa. 37:36), Jesus' point about the angelic forces at his disposal is easy to see. In the Bible, angels are holy, powerful, and busy servants! No wonder the Psalms say that God "makes his angels winds, and his ministers a flame of fire" (Heb. 1:7).

---

3 Q&A 16. *The Confessions of Our Faith* (Glasgow, Scotland, Free Presbyterian Publications, 1958), 135–136.

While angels were created holy, they were "subject to change" (WLC 16)—and change some did! The catechism says, "God by his providence permitted some of the angels, willfully and irreversibly, to fall into sin and damnation" (WLC 19). Scripture refers to "angels who did not stay within their own position of authority, but left their proper dwelling" and are now "kept in eternal chains under gloomy darkness until the judgment" (Jude 6).

WHAT DOES THIS HAVE TO DO WITH SATAN?

John writes that the devil "has been sinning from the beginning" (1 John 3:8) and Jesus says that Satan was "a murderer from the beginning" (John 8:44). "The beginning" refers to God's creation of the visible world (Gen. 1:1; John 1:1). Satan was already wicked in the beginning, which shows that his origin is with the holy angelic order that God created *before* the world existed.

Satan was created good, but he was among those angels who fell away from God. Perhaps this was due to pride. Paul may be referring to this when he warns against hastily electing a man as an elder in the church, noting the special danger that accompanies a new believer suddenly entrusted with authority: "He must not be a recent convert, or he may become puffed up with conceit and fall into the condemnation of the devil" (1 Tim. 3:6 ESV). Whatever the cause of Satan's fall, Jesus speaks of God's victory over this creature saying, "I saw Satan fall like lightning from heaven" (Luke 10:17 ESV). He's recalling the moment Satan's rebellion against God failed and he was cast out of heaven.

Where did Satan come from? He came from God. Beyond this, neither the Old or New Testaments offer any specifics about the devil's origin or the reason for his rebellion. This is a mystery known only to God.

Satan was created as a glorious angel but became a rebel against God. Now, he's beyond redemption's reach. While that leaves many unanswered questions for us, the Bible isn't silent about the devil's identity, activity, and destiny.

THE DEVIL IN THE OLD TESTAMENT

Satan isn't mentioned often in the Old Testament. He's named in Job 1–2, where he's one of "the sons of God" appearing before God to report on what's happening on the earth; in 1 Chronicles 21:1, where he entices David into ordering a census of Israel; and in Zechariah 3:1–2, where he appears before God to make accusations against God's servant Joshua, high priest in the time of Nehemiah. The mention of demons is even more rare, though we do encounter references to "evil spirits," notably in association with King Saul (1 Kings 16:14) and in connection with the worship of idols (Deut. 32:17; Ps. 106:37).

Even though those are the only places in the Old Testament we see Satan referred to by name, that doesn't mean they're the only places he makes an appearance. Genesis 3 contains the tragic narrative of humankind's rebellion against God. There, we read of a serpent that "was more cunning than any animal of the field which the Lord God had made" (Gen. 3:1). This serpent beguiles Eve. He questions her and levies accusations against God, tempting Eve to believe his lies. Eve "took and ate" the forbidden fruit and shared it with Adam, who ate some also, in full knowledge of what he was doing (Gen. 3:6). Adam's sin plunged himself, his bride, all their posterity, and all of creation into fear, shame, death, and alienation from God (Gen. 3:7–24; Rom. 5:12; 8:20–23).

Christian scholars usually see Satan's tempting, deceiving presence behind the scenes of this encounter, animating the words and actions of the serpent. There are good reasons for this. In Revelation, we find this reference to Satan's demise: "And the great dragon was thrown down, the serpent of old who is called the devil and Satan, who deceives the whole world; he was thrown down to the earth, and his angels were thrown down with him" (Rev. 12:9). Later we read virtually the same words, "And he took hold of the dragon, the serpent of old, who is the devil and Satan, and bound him for a thousand years" (Rev. 20:2).

In addition, Paul writes to the Corinthian Christians about his concern that they might be led away from their faithfulness to Christ, referring to the events of Genesis 3: "But I am afraid that, as the serpent deceived Eve by his trickery, your minds will be led astray from sincere and pure devotion to Christ" (2 Cor. 11:3). He goes on to remind them that the danger lies in the devil's deception of the church through false teachers. "Satan disguises himself as an angel of light," Paul writes, "Therefore it is not surprising if his servants also disguise themselves as servants of righteousness, whose end will be according to their deeds" (2 Cor. 11:13–15).

Most significantly, however, is the way God speaks to the serpent in Genesis 3. He puts "enmity" between the seed of the woman and the seed of the serpent that will end with the heel of the woman's seed being "bruised" as the head of the serpent is "crushed" (Gen. 3:15). With these words, God declares war on Satan. The serpent will not hold onto the woman's allegiance. Rather, God will preserve a people for himself—a faithful seed from which the offspring of the woman will one day rise to destroy the serpent and his followers forever. This is often considered the first promise of the gospel in the Bible, and it unfolds in the rest of the biblical narrative of God's redemption of sinners and creation. There can be no doubt about how this influenced Jesus' saving mission and the ultimate outcome of his grace in our lives. "The Son of God appeared for this purpose, to destroy the works of the devil," writes

John (1 John 3:8). Paul closes his great epistle to the Romans with the stunning benediction, "The God of peace will soon crush Satan under your feet" (Rom. 16:20).

THE DEVIL AND DEMONS IN THE GOSPELS AND ACTS

Unlike the Old Testament, where Satan mostly works "off-stage," the New Testament is full of dramatic encounters between Satan and Christ. The New Testament is replete with references to the devil, Satan, demons, and forces of darkness. It also introduces new names like Beelzebub, Belial, and "the prince of the power of the air" (Matt. 12:24; 2 Cor. 6:15; Eph. 2:1–3). What's behind this explosion of satanic activity? What do all these new names and terms mean?

Most of the unfamiliar names for the devil in the Gospels entered the discourse of the Jewish culture during the time between the testaments. Books like *Jubilees, War Scroll, Rule of the Community, Baba Bathra, 1 Enoch,* and *The Wisdom of Solomon* were not considered Scripture by most Jews, but they were highly regarded. In these books, we first encounter names like Belial. Beelzebub, however—"Lord of the Flies"— dates back to a Philistine god mentioned in 2 Kings 1:2. Jesus refers to him as Satan in Luke 11:18.

We also note the widespread activity of demons, invisible beings who seem to be described as the "angels" that follow the devil (Matt. 25:41). In the apocryphal Jewish book of *Jubilees,* the demons emerge as the survivors of a great judgment against them after they seduced "the daughters of men," a reference to the Nephilim—the renowned pre-flood giants of Genesis 6:1–4.[4] These survivors continue to stand with

---

4   See the FAQ in chapter 4 for more about the Nephilim.

Satan to accomplish his mission in the world. Whatever their origin, demons are clearly vicious agents of the devil who do all they can to harm people. They possess people not only in distant gentile regions like the Decapolis (Mark 5:1–20) but also in Jewish areas like Capernaum. Here, Mark writes, Jesus first encounters a demon and casts it out of a possessed person (Mark 1:21–29).

In the New Testament we find almost 80 references to Satan or the devil(s), and their activity is described in detail. Looking first to the Gospels, we should pay attention to the ways the devil and demons sought to undermine Jesus and his mission; harm people in physical, spiritual, and psychological ways; take possession of people's bodies and control their faculties; and rob people of the gospel that Jesus proclaimed. Here are some examples:

- » He tempts Jesus to disobey his Father and abandon his mission (Matt. 4:1–11; Luke 4:1–14).

- » Through Peter, he tries to dissuade Jesus from going to Jerusalem to die (Matt. 16:23).

- » He enters the heart of Judas Iscariot and entices him to betray Jesus (Luke 22:3; John 13:27).

- » He "binds" a woman, causing her to suffer with physical illness for many years (Luke 13:16).

- » He snatches away from hearts the seed of the word sown by Jesus (Matt. 13:18; Mark 4:15).

- » He is a murderer and the father of lies (John 8:44–45).

When we consider the many ways Satan tries to destroy people, we can be thankful that Christ has come to liberate and "[heal] all who were oppressed by the devil" (Acts 10:38).

The prayer Jesus gives to his disciples, commonly called The Lord's Prayer, begins with the petition, "Thy Kingdom come," and concludes with, "Deliver us from evil" (Matt. 6:9–13). Jesus' conquest over the evil one and his attendants is directly tied to the coming of Christ's kingdom. "If I cast out demons by the finger of God, then the Kingdom of God has come upon you," Jesus says (Luke 11:20). Jesus' ministry is characterized by his "teaching in the synagogues and proclaiming the gospel of the Kingdom and healing every disease and every affliction," including the healing of "those oppressed by demons" (Matt. 4:23–24).

When Christ the King brought his dominion to this world, the demons who had been hiding in the shadows for centuries were exposed by the light of his coming. He banished them from their parasitical dwellings. Jesus went on not only to liberate oppressed people from these sinister spirits but also to overthrow Satan himself through the power of his death and resurrection.

Historically speaking, Jesus' power over demons is one of the most clearly attested aspects of his ministry, no matter how embarrassing this may be to sophisticated intellectuals of the 21st century who prefer to dismiss the idea of demons as they would garden fairies and leprechauns. Even disbelieving historians note that Jesus' power of exorcism was so great and the healings attributed to this power so attractive that his opponents, unable to deny their reality, resorted to accusing him of doing this work through the power of Satan, a charge Jesus easily dismissed.[5] In other words, if we wish to take Jesus seriously, we will also have to

---

5   Marcus Borg, *Jesus, A New Vision* (London: SPCK, 1987), 60–65.

take seriously his view of demons and the devil, together with his ministry to liberate people from their malicious influence.

The ministry of Jesus was extended in the world through his apostles, and we read of their ministries in the book of Acts. Here we especially see the work of Peter and Paul highlighted, learning how God used them to expand the work of the gospel not only in Judea but more broadly into the gentile world. As the reach of the mission grew larger and took in people and cities whose only experience of religion was the worship of idols, the apostles would encounter Satanic opposition and conflict.

First, we see Paul confronting a sorcerer early in his first mission. He refers to this opponent as a "son of the devil," and "enemy of all righteousness," cursing him with blindness as a sign of Jesus' victory over the darkness of evil (Acts 13:6–12). In Philippi, we read of Paul exorcising a demon from a possessed slave girl being trafficked by her owners because of her psychic powers (Acts 16:16–24). Through Paul's ministry, the gospel took hold so strongly in the ancient city of Ephesus—famous for its worship of Artemis in her Temple, one of the wonders of the ancient world—that its converted citizens abandoned their occult practices, burning their books and materials, a conflagration worth about 5000 days' wages by today's standards. The power to liberate demonically oppressed people through the power of the name of Jesus was already well-known in many circles (Acts 19:14ff) and this increased the attractiveness of the faith for many.

THE DEVIL AND DEMONS IN THE EPISTLES

In the remaining chapters of this booklet, we'll take a deeper look at how the apostles describe Satan, his allies, and Jesus' triumph over them, as well as how Christian believers continue to engage with wicked spiritual forces. We'll look at Satan's strategies to hinder the spread of the gospel, harass God's servants, tempt believers into sin, deceive believers with lies, and shame believers with accusations. But in this 30,000-foot view of the Bible's teaching on the subject, let's note a few central themes regarding Satan's efforts to slow the progress of the gospel and attack Christian people and churches.

1. Blinding Unbelievers

In 2 Corinthians 4:4, Paul writes that Satan, whom he describes as "the god of this age," blinds the minds of unbelievers to the beauty of Jesus, the danger of their sinfulness, and the wonders of the gospel.

2. Animating Unbelievers

In Ephesians 2:2, Paul writes that Satan, whom he calls "the prince of the power of the air"—a common title at the time in that part of the world—is working in people who are not followers of Christ, those he refers to as "the sons of disobedience among we all once lived." While he goes on to say that our battle is not with people but with the "powers" and "spiritual forces of wickedness" (Eph 6:10ff), he doesn't hesitate to note that before we follow Christ, we are under the influence of Satan, often carrying out his will without even knowing it. Persecution, for instance, is carried out by people, but we bless and pray for persecutors because we know an enslaving darkness controls them.

3. Exploiting Our Sins and Weaknesses

Also in Ephesians, Paul urges Christians, "Do not let the sun do down on your anger, and do not give the devil an opportunity" (Eph. 4:26–27). He knows that when we remain sinfully angry, we leave open doors through which the devil would like to come and create more havoc.

4. Sending Temptations

In 1 Corinthians 7:5, Paul reminds married believers that they should not refrain from sexual union with one another for extended periods of time so that "Satan will not tempt you because of your lack of self-control." This principle applies to far more than sexual temptation. When we're in a place of vulnerability and our "flesh is weak," we're more likely to succumb to the enticements that our first parents Adam and Eve couldn't resist. If they fell away when they were perfect, we should be humble and wise enough to admit that we—imperfect and living in a fallen world—are vulnerable to any number of temptations which could be presented to us.

5. Physical, Psychological, and Spiritual Attacks

In 2 Corinthians 12:7, Paul writes about his "thorn in the flesh, a messenger of Satan to torment me." There's much speculation about what this thorn was. Whether it was a physical illness, persecution, or even a form of psychological distress, it was certainly from Satan. And rather than delivering him from it, God preserves Paul despite it. Three times Paul asked God to remove this satanic messenger, but God refused Paul's request saying, "My grace is sufficient for you" (2 Cor. 12:9). In a similar way, Jesus told Peter, "Satan has demanded to sift you men like wheat" (Luke 22:31). Jesus doesn't stop this from occurring. Instead, by his gracious intercession, he preserves Peter despite his failure and restores him. We don't know exactly why God chooses to sometimes allow Satan to prevail over his servants in this way, but we can be sure of sufficient grace to accompany us in the ordeal and his intercession to renew us despite our many weaknesses.

6. Hindering Gospel Ministry

In 1 Thessalonians 2:17–18, Paul tells the Thessalonian Christians that he wanted to visit them but "Satan hindered us."[6] Paul doesn't say exactly

---

6   This is a curious observation that Paul makes, one we should take seriously. Sometimes we're not able to discern whether we're being hindered by the enemy (and we have no choice but to accept the situation) or being restrained and redirected by the Lord. The issue when that occurs isn't struggling to try to figure out the difference, but trusting in God's providence. That the devil is involved in something doesn't mean that God is not ultimately in control of the situation. We can rest in God's sovereignty and say that "due to the hurricane (or pandemic!) we have been providentially hindered from making that mission trip." There are

how Satan did that, but whether it was a lack of resources to make the trip, illness, distracting demands elsewhere, or the absence of safe transport, Paul saw Satan's hand behind what was happening.

7. False Teaching and Deception

In 2 Corinthians 11:1–6, Paul warns the church about false teachers who appear to be God's servants but who are in fact deceivers, leading them away from the truth. He compares these false teachers to Satan himself and their tactics to those the serpent used to entice Eve.

There are many malicious "schemes of the devil" (Eph. 6:10–20) against which Christians must arm themselves and for which they must prepare. But while we're to "be on the alert" because the devil is a prowling lion looking for lunch (1 Pet. 5:8), the apostles are equally clear that in all of these assaults, Christ will ultimately lead us into his victory over the darkness and that "neither . . . angels, nor principalities . . . nor powers . . . can separate us from the love of God that is in Christ Jesus our Lord" (Rom. 8:37–39). Paul assures the Thessalonians, "The Lord is faithful, and He will strengthen and protect you from the evil one" (2 Thess. 3:3). The writer of Hebrews declares that God the Son became incarnate as the Lord Jesus Christ "so that through death He might destroy the one who has the power of death, that is, the devil" (Heb. 2:14). Because of Jesus' victory over the devil, we can now "Submit . . . to God . . . resist the devil, and he will flee from you" (James 4:7).

Let's turn now to look at how our Lord and Savior Jesus Christ defeated the devil and his powers, how the Christian and the church persevere in that victory now through faith, and what we can anticipate in the future about the ultimate outcome of our struggle against the devil and his forces.

---

many things in the realm of the invisible creation that we're not privileged to see or understand—at least, not yet.

"So that through death He might destroy the one who has the power of death, that is, the devil."

Hebrews 2:14

CHAPTER TWO

The Devil's Defeat

WHEN GOD SAYS TO THE SERPENT, "I will put enmity between you and the woman, and between your offspring and her offspring; he shall bruise you on the head, and you shall bruise his heel" (Gen. 3:15 ESV), he declares war against evil. He declares his intention to crush the serpent and restore all that was lost in the fall of humankind. Carrying out this mission, Jesus came to defeat the devil and overthrow every horrid thing he'd accomplished in the world. John writes, "The Son of God appeared for this purpose, to destroy the works of the devil" (1 John 3:8).

We should be clear about the fact that *God declared this war.* God is the one on the offensive, establishing the enmity and pressing the conflict. He's not merely seeking to retain some territory from a dangerous usurper. Rather, God mounts an offensive to redeem his sons and daughters. This reaches its promised fulfillment in the coming of Jesus into the world announcing the gospel of the Kingdom. *Gospel* comes from an ancient word translated as victory: The message of Jesus is about his victory over the devil, dark powers, and death.

CHRIST THE CONQUEROR

We often think about Christ's redeeming work in legal terms. Instead of being declared "guilty" in the courtroom, we're found to be righteous because Christ's death in our place pays the penalty our sin deserves.

His righteousness is credited to us as if it's our own. This is justification—how we're made right with God. But this doesn't exhaust the meaning of Christ's death. On the cross, Christ is revealed as both our substitute and the conqueror who defeats death and the devil. Like King David, Jesus runs to the battle to face the giant who wants to make us his slaves. With a great blow to his enemy's head, Christ liberates the people of God (see the story of David's defeat of Goliath in 1 Sam. 17).

This is sometimes referred to as "Christus Victor." Christ came as the champion of God's people to defeat their enemies: death and sin. This view of Christ as conqueror demonstrates that God's great deliverance of his people took into account the fullness of our fallenness. Not only does God remove our guilt, but he also overcomes our alienation from him by uniting us to himself in Christ, reconciling us to himself in love, and then liberating us from the enslaving forces of the devil and death by destroying them at the cross. Justification, adoption, and liberation are all aspects of the saving work of Jesus.

THE KING ON THE ATTACK

When Jesus came into the world as Savior, God launched the invasion to overthrow the power of death and evil. The Bible's narrative is not that Satan was attacking Jesus, but rather that Jesus goes on the attack against Satan, and he's determined to conquer him completely. Not only this, but the people of God share in the victory of Christ over evil. We're summoned to "overcome" (Rev. 2–3), called "more than conquerors through [Christ] who loves us" (Rom. 8:37 ESV), and rejoice that the Savior "always leads us in triumph" (2 Cor. 2:14). Far from cowering in fear, those who follow Christ may approach the archenemy of their souls with faith in Christ, his word, and his blood shed on their behalf. "They overcame . . . because of the blood of the Lamb and because of the word of their testimony, and they did not love their life even when faced death" (Rev. 12:11).

Moreover, we confess Christ's prevailing power in our lives when we're confronted by dark forces:

> What then shall we say to these things? If God is for us, who can be against us? . . . Who shall separate us from the love of Christ? Shall tribulation, or distress, or persecution, or famine, or nakedness, or danger, or sword? As it is written, "For your sake we are being killed all the day long; we are regarded as sheep to be slaughtered." No, in all these things we are more than conquerors through him who loved us. For I am sure that neither death nor life, nor angels nor rulers, nor things present nor things to come, nor powers, nor height nor depth, nor anything else in all creation, will be able to separate us from the love of God in Christ Jesus our Lord. (Rom. 8:31–39 ESV)

These words have strengthened believers for two thousand years. They remind us that the love of God and the grace of Christ are infinitely more powerful than any attack Satan might mount against us. In these passages, we see the reality that our Savior is the Lord of Hosts, the Commander of the Angelic armies of heaven that march on our behalf and speed to our service.

There's a troubling aspect to this truth in our experience, however. We read of Christ's victory over and destruction of the devil, and yet we also read of the ongoing battle believers have with dark forces arrayed against humanity and the church. We read of Satan on the prowl seeking to deceive, devastate, and rob people of life, peace, beauty, and God's word. In our lives, we can see the terrible consequences of the work of these enemies, not only in the power of the indwelling sin we all feel and seek to resist, but in the high cost of sin in our families, societies, and churches. The violence of our world; the horror of war; the stories of disaster, murder, sexual abuse and the despoiling of creation that fill our news cycle; and the all-too-familiar scenes of starvation and slavery add to this picture of apparently unrestrained evil and misery.

How can we confess that Christ has defeated the devil when we can clearly see that he is at work in dreadful ways? How does our view that Christ has conquered stand up in the face of the entire catalog of human woe? The answer to this question lies in grasping the various stages of the devil's defeat and understanding the language the Bible employs to describe his conquest.

STAGES OF THE CONQUEST

There are seven stages of Christ's victory that span the pages of the Bible, from Genesis to Revelation:

> *Stage One: Christ's Victory Promised*
> *Stage Two: Christ's Victory Initiated*
> *Stage Three: Christ's Victory Achieved*
> *Stage Four: Christ's Victory Announced*
> *Stage Five: Christ's Victory Unfolded*
> *Stage Six: Christ's Victory Consummated*
> *Stage Seven: Christ's Victory Celebrated*

These seven stages of Christ's triumph over Satan help us grasp the scale of the devil's activity and the scope of Jesus' mission. These identify how God has already worked in history, where things currently stand in the campaign, and what we can expect in the future. Let's take a brief look at them in succession.

1. Christ's Victory Promised

As we've seen, God promises to redeem his people and defeat the serpent immediately after the fall (Gen. 3:15). This promise continues to expand across the narrative that unfolds in the Old Testament, focusing after the flood on Abraham and the great family of Israel that emerged from his descendants Isaac and Jacob.

Towards the end of Abraham's life, after his faith received its greatest test, the Angel of the Lord repeated to Abraham the words of the covenant that God had spoken to him decades earlier, but then added a vital phrase: "Your seed shall possess the gate of their enemies" (Gen. 22:17). A descendant of the father of Israel was destined to bless the gentiles and conquer the enemies of God's people.

Through the eras of the exodus and conquest, of the judges and kings, and down through the prophets who by their songs, visions, dreams, and predictions spoke of the coming one who would be Israel's Messiah and the Savior of the gentiles, the boundaries of the promise grew. God's people were prisoners of hope, waiting for the king to enter the holy city and free them from their oppressors. The glories of the promised messiah and his kingdom were Israel's hope—and the hope of the world. God had promised to send the Messiah, the seed of the woman, the descendent of Seth, the Seed of Abraham, the Son of David, the Servant of the Lord, the Son of Man, who would receive the kingdom and redeem the people of God. *How long must we wait?* the people of Israel often wondered as they endured sorrows, exile, and, even when back in their land, the domination of exploitative and violent powers from Greece and Rome. *How long?*

Then a mysterious, new star appeared on the horizon and caught the eye of Persian sages. The entire Old Testament contained the promise and the day of its fulfillment was dawning.

2. Christ's Victory Initiated

The incarnation of God the Son occurred with his conception in Mary's womb and birth in Bethlehem. The Magi came to adore him, stopping in Jerusalem and asking Herod for the whereabouts of the newly born "King of the Jews" (Matt. 2:2). Herod, a powerful and notoriously violent ruler, passed along what the court theologians told him—the Messiah will be born in Bethlehem according to the promise of Micah the prophet (Matt. 2:4–6). The king added, "when you have found Him, report to me, so that I too may come and worship Him" (Matt. 2:8). He planned to murder the newborn to protect his throne from an upstart usurper. The Magi found the infant savior in Bethlehem, but they never went back to see Herod (Matt. 2:12). His plan foiled by the Magi's getaway, Herod initiated a murderous rampage against all the male infants in Bethlehem. After being warned by an angel, Joseph took Mary and Jesus to Egypt for shelter. Jesus the Savior was saved from the sword of Herod's troops (Matt. 2:13–15).

The violence of Jesus' infant years isn't shocking when we consider the implications of his arrival for his opponents. On numerous occasions in the Old Testament era of promise, the serpent sought to snuff out the messianic line and prevent the birth of the one who would crush his head. Satan didn't succeed, but with the savior's arrival in the world, the devil would pull out all the stops in a desperate effort to thwart the coming of God's kingdom.

After Jesus was baptized by John at the Jordan River, the Spirit descended on him and led him into the wilderness of Judea. There he met the devil in what appears to be their first face-to-face confrontation. Satan set three temptations before Jesus in hopes that he would yield, surrendering the fight for the world. The serpent saw a weakened man, hungry and alone; perhaps he thought he'd be easy prey since Adam, the first "son of God," yielded to him even when he was surrounded by food, accompanied by his beautiful bride, and living in a sinless paradise. But Jesus didn't yield for a moment. Instead, he drove the devil away from him through the power of the Scriptures. Three times Jesus quoted from Deuteronomy, the history of Israel in the wilderness, rebuking the enemy's advances and letting him know that where Adam and Israel had failed, he would conquer. Then Satan "left him until an opportune time" (Luke 4:13).

The wilderness temptation was the beginning of Jesus' fight on our behalf: his Satan-resisting battle that would lead to his Satan-conquering triumph. This battle would rage for three more years. During his earthly ministry, Jesus liberated people from demonic powers and announced, "If I cast out demons by the finger of God, then the Kingdom of God has come upon you" (Luke 11:20). In Acts, Peter summarizes Jesus' entire life and ministry, recalling "You know of Jesus of Nazareth, how God anointed Him with the Holy Spirit and with power, and how He went about doing good and healing all who were oppressed by the devil, for God was with him" (Acts 10:38). He healed the sick, raised the dead, exorcised demons, and purified the Temple, all pointing to his mission to overthrow the darkness as the one who is the "Light of the world" (John 8:12; Acts 10:38) He came as a strong deliverer to "plunder" the devil's house, to "bind the strongman" and rescue those under his enslaving ownership (Mark 3:26–27).

As Jesus' ministry advanced across Galilee and Judea, the darkness was in retreat. His apostles also went out preaching, healing, and casting out demons. The light was growing brighter every day. Jesus then "set his face" to go to Jerusalem (Luke 9:51), establishing a course leading to an ultimate battle with the devil, the powers, and the human forces in politics and religion that served Satan's ends. At stake was the glory of God, the liberation of humanity, and the renewal of the cosmos. Jesus entered Jerusalem as the long-promised and hoped-for king—the people acknowledged him as Messiah with shouts of "Hosanna to the Son of David!" and cast palm branches and cloaks before him (Zech. 9; Matt. 21:1–12). The Gospels record that the whole city was stirred. So was hell.

3. Christ's Victory Achieved

During that climactic week in Jerusalem, Jesus referred to Satan three times as the "prince of the world" who would "come," be "driven out," and at last "condemned" (John 12:31; 14:30; 16:11). The dark forces unleashed a final effort to destroy Jesus and annihilate any hope of salvation for humanity. His arrest signaled that his opponents had the upper hand, at least temporarily—it was "your hour, and the power of darkness" (Luke 22:53 ESV), he said to them. Satan entered the heart of Judas (Luke 22:3–6) and was given permission to "sift" Peter like wheat (Luke 22:31). Judas betrayed Christ; Peter violently defended Jesus and then denied him in cowardice.

Arrested and beaten, Jesus was subjected to a mockery of a trial filled with contradictory testimony and false accusations. Handed over to the Romans, he was whipped and beaten, mocked and ridiculed, and finally— at the behest of a mob screaming for his blood—was led away to a hill just outside the city and crucified between two criminals, suffering the most gruesome form of execution available to the powers of the time. In the course of a week, Jesus went from welcomed deliverer and king to condemned false prophet. When he breathed his last on that Friday afternoon, all hope appeared to die with him.

Perhaps no one has better captured the despair of that moment than C.S. Lewis in his description of Aslan's death on the Stone Table. Having given his life in exchange for a boy named Edmund, Aslan is muzzled, his mane shaved off, bound with cords and bereft of friends. He looks silently to the heavens as the witch hisses in his ear, "Understand that you have given me Narnia forever. You have lost your own life and you have not saved his. In that knowledge, despair and die."[1]

The Pevensie sisters nearby weep over the death of their great friend. They can't begin to understand why he would yield to such horrors when he could've ended the disaster with a single swipe of his massive paw. Their tears reflect those of the women who stood beneath the cross of Jesus as he died.

They were not the only ones who didn't understand. A few decades later Paul wrote, "None of the rulers of this age understood this, for if they had, they would not have crucified the Lord of glory" (1 Cor. 2:8). Behind the scenes of a dying man crying out with a parched tongue protruding from swollen, bleeding lips, a battle was raging—and the crucified man was conquering his foes, and ours.

One of the clearest descriptions of the crucifixion as God's victory over Satan is Colossians 2:13–15:

> When you were dead in your sins and in the uncircumcision of your flesh, God made you alive with Christ. He forgave us all our sins, having canceled the charge of our legal indebtedness, which stood against us and condemned us; he has taken it away, nailing it to the cross. And having disarmed the powers and authorities, he made a public spectacle of them, triumphing over them by the cross.

God disarmed and debased the principalities and powers, "triumphing over them by the cross." The moment when Satan and his forces thought they'd defeated the seed of the woman, bruising him on the heel, was precisely the moment that the battle turned. F.F. Bruce writes, "As he was suspended there, bound hand and foot to the wood in apparent

---

1   C.S. Lewis, *The Lion, the Witch, and the Wardrobe* (United Kingdom: HarperCollins, 2005), 161.

weakness, they (the powers) imagined they had him at their mercy, and flung themselves upon him with hostile intent . . . but he grappled with them and mastered them."[2] This is why we're those who overcome by the blood of the Lamb (Rev. 12:11); the death of Jesus is our victory over death and the devil.

4. Christ's Victory Announced

The resurrection is sometimes referred to as Christ's victory, and in a certain sense that's true. But it's true only because it's tied to his death for us and his triumph over the evil one. As we've noted, the cross was the ultimate battle for the souls of humanity and the creation itself. On Golgotha, "the place of the skull", Jesus the seed of the woman crushed the serpent's head. The resurrection was God's announcement to the disciples and the world that death and the devil were defeated, that Christ "through death . . . [destroyed] the one who has the power of death, that is, the devil" (Heb. 2:14).

When Christ died and rose again, he became supreme over death and the grave. "Do not be afraid," Jesus said to John on Patmos, "I am the first and the last, and the living One; I was dead, and behold, I am alive forevermore, and I have the keys of death and Hades" (Rev. 1:17–18). This is why Paul also describes death as a defeated foe: "Death has been swallowed up in victory. Where, O death, is your victory? Where, O death is your sting?" (1 Cor. 15:54–55). The resurrection of Jesus Christ is the visible testimony of God to the powers, the apostles, to us, and to the world, that Christ has gained the victory over the devil and death. We need not fear death or the devil any longer, as both are defeated foes. John Stott writes, "The cross was the victory won and the resurrection the victory endorsed, proclaimed and demonstrated."[3]

---

2   F. F. Bruce, *The Epistles to the Colossians, to Philemon, and to the Ephesians* (United Kingdom: Eerdmans Publishing Company, 1984),148.

3   John Stott, *The Cross Of Christ* (Downers Grove, Illinois: IVP, 1985), 231.

From this moment on, the powers are described as being under the feet of the sovereign savior (Eph. 1:20–23).

5. Christ's Victory Unfolded

After ascending to the throne of heaven, Jesus pours out the Spirit upon his church on the Day of Pentecost. This signals the new era of the Spirit's work to glorify Jesus Christ as his people proclaim the gospel (Acts 1:8; 2:1–11). Peter's message that day saw some three thousand respond to the astonishing news of what God had done in the cross and resurrection, and Acts unfolds the remarkable story of the faith spreading like flame as it takes root in Jerusalem and reaches the farthest corners of the known world. Thousands receive both new life and a commission to take the news of Jesus' victory to the gentile world. Later, Jesus tells Paul "to open their eyes, so that they may turn from darkness to light and from the power of Satan to God, that they may receive forgiveness of sins and a place among those who are sanctified by faith in me" (Acts 26:18). Did you catch his reference to Satan and conversion? To become a Christian is to be rescued from Satan's power and move from the darkness into the light. While we can make Star Wars jokes about joining the "Dark Side," Christian conversion really does mean we leave the darkness for the kingdom of Jesus where we share in the inheritance of the "saints in light" (Col. 1:12–14).

To this day, every new gospel-preaching church planted, every new birth of the soul, and every penetration of the gospel into new regions reveals the unfolding of Christ's victory at the cross.

6. Christ's Victory Consummated

Just as Israel longed for the birth of the Messiah, Christians long for the return of the Messiah. It's been awhile! In a certain way, to become a Christian is to be ushered into a waiting room. In conversion, we become those who have "turned to God from idols to serve a living and true

God, and to wait for His Son from heaven, whom He raised from the dead, that is, Jesus who rescues us from the wrath to come" (1 Thess. 1:9–10). I'm not an especially patient person and many days I wish Christ would return and put an end to the misery so many continue to endure (or just get me out of the trouble I'm in!). We long for that day not only because we'll see the beauty of our Savior's face, but because we know at that moment he'll make "all things new" (Rev. 21:5).

In one sense, we've already been raised from the dead to new life, but we also know that the resurrection of the body—the abolition of the presence of death—awaits this final day. We've been raised from the dead already so that we shall be raised from the dead eternally and bodily (John 5:28, 29–30). We groan under the weight of death while we wait, grieving, but not as those "who have no hope" (1 Thess. 4:13). We believe that those who have gone ahead of us are not lost, and all of us will together meet with and be with the Lord.

Creation also joins us in longing for this day, "groaning" to be finally liberated from its continued limitations and decay due to sin (Rom. 8:20–25). In hurricanes, earthquakes, tsunamis, and tornadoes; in wars, rumors of wars, and societal upheavals; and in the persecutions the people of God endure, we await the day that Christ returns and his victory is complete. On that day, Scripture says, the devil who deceived them was thrown into the lake of fire and brimstone . . . Then Death and Hades were thrown into the lake of fire. This is the second death, the lake of fire" (Rev. 20:10–14). This moment, when Death is hurled into the Lake of Fire, will mark the consummation of Christ's victory begun in his death and resurrection. "The last enemy to be destroyed is death" (1 Cor. 15:26 ESV), writes Paul, a man who would die at the hands of Roman executioners. Did he think that Satan had won the day when he lost his life? Not at all. His vision of Christ the King who has won the victory gave him faith to face death with hope in the Savior. He knew the day would come when death will be swallowed up in victory (1 Cor. 15:54).

We don't know where we are in this part of the story of Christ's victory over the devil. We may be near to Christ's return, or it may be centuries or millennia away in the future. God, after all, is not impatient and doesn't count time as we do. He waits for the full harvest and doesn't wish that any should perish (2 Pet. 3:9). He longs for his great and final banquet to be a standing-room-only function (Luke 14:12–24). So, whether we see Christ return or enter his presence by death, we live in unashamed hope (Ps. 119:116; Rom. 5:5) and look "for the appearing of the glory of our great God and Savior, Chris Jesus" (Titus 2:13). We hasten that day by remaining faithful to the Lord, proclaiming his victory in the world, and resisting the devil when he sends temptation, deception, accusation, or fear our way.

7. Christ's Victory Celebrated

The beauty of our inheritance in heaven is described as a banquet at which we rejoice in the greatness and grace of God our savior. In that celebration, our mourning is turned into dancing, and every tear is wiped away. The feast of the kingdom is described as an eternal celebration of Jesus' marriage to his glorified bride, the church:

> Then I heard what seemed to be the voice of a great multitude, like the roar of many waters and like the sound of mighty peals of thunder, crying out, "Hallelujah! For the Lord our God the Almighty reigns. Let us rejoice and exult and give him the glory, for the marriage of the Lamb has come, and his Bride has made herself ready; it was granted her to clothe herself with fine linen, bright and pure"—for the fine linen is the righteous deeds of the saints. And the angel said to me, "Write this: Blessed are those who are invited to the marriage supper of the Lamb." And he said to me, "These are the true words of God." (Rev. 19:6–9 ESV)

Until Christ returns, the church celebrates the Lord's Supper to remember his sacrifice on our behalf, to proclaim his death—his victory over the devil and death!—and to participate in that victory as we feast on all of the benefits of his life, death, and resurrection. We eat and drink at the Lord's Table in commemoration of the cross of Christ and in anticipation of the final celebration of the victory of Christ: "But thanks be to God, who gives us the victory through our Lord Jesus Christ" (1 Cor. 15:57).

Having seen these various stages in Christ's triumph over the devil and his allies, we need to next consider how these impact our current experience of his work in the world, our hearts, and the church. This is especially true when it comes to how we face the challenges presented by indwelling sin, temptations, deception, and suffering. How does the victory of Jesus at the cross change the way we live right now as we wait for the full and final overthrow of Satan to occur? That is the subject of our next chapter.

"Stand firm therefore."

Ephesians 6:14

CHAPTER THREE

Resisting the Devil

ON OCTOBER 30, 1938, a great panic seized thousands of people in the United States as they heard the Mercury Theater broadcast production of H.G. Wells' *War of the Worlds.* The performance, narrated by actor Orson Welles, was so persuasive that many thought an actual alien invasion had taken place and that New York and other major American cities were being overrun by Martian forces. Despite announcements that it was just a play, hysteria gripped the minds of many who heard the broadcast, leading to attempts by police to break into the studio and stop the show. Later, to calls for greater federal regulation of radio programming.

By way of contrast, on December 7, 1941, despite repeated warnings from Navy Intelligence Officers, the U.S. Naval Base at a sleepy and peaceful Pearl Harbor in Hawaii was attacked by the Imperial Forces of Japan, resulting in thousands of deaths and leading to America's entry into World War II. Donald Goldstein's book, *At Dawn, We Slept: The Untold Story of Pearl Harbor,* narrates the tale of America's lack of preparation for the attack.

In the first case, people panicked over a mythical war, and in the second, they ignored a real war about to break upon them. When it comes to our battles with spiritual forces, we can't make the same mistakes. While we give glory to God alone, we also need to give the devil his due and make sure we're "on the alert" for his assaults. As Paul noted, we must be prepared "so that no advantage would be taken of us by Satan, for we are not ignorant of his schemes" (2 Cor. 2:11). This is no mythical war, and we'd best be ready.

THE REALITY OF THE BATTLE

We've considered what the Scriptures say about the devil, looking at his origin and power, along with his nature and intent. We've also recalled how Christ has conquered Satan through the cross. Now we need to look carefully at how we live between the cross and Christ's final triumph at history's conclusion. How do we live for God's glory, seeking to please him, all the while taking seriously Satan's opposition to Christ's church? And how do we avoid any sense of terror about his activity?

All around us and deep within us we see the ravages of sin. We note the tracks of our treacherous foe in the headlines of our sin-shattered world. Do we acknowledge this reality as we should? We really are in a battle and this is why Christians are called to be those who "overcome" (Rev. 2:7) and why Paul exhorts us to be well trained in the "weapons of righteousness for the right hand and the left" (2 Cor. 6:7); apparently this struggle is so great that we must become ambidextrous fighters rather than weekend warriors who view our enemy with a sense of casual dismissal.

While some may over-spiritualize their everyday experiences ("An angel helped me get a parking place"), it's also true that we can under-spiritualize our experiences in the face of evil ("That's just the way things are"). As we've seen, the apostles' deep trust in God's providential guidance of their lives and their firm reliance on Christ's power didn't mean they ignored the threat of Satan's mischief. They knew he was at work to stop them. But they didn't believe that his activity, even his violent opposition, would ultimately succeed. With Job, they would say of God, "no purpose of yours can be thwarted" (Job 42:2 ESV). Paul boldly confessed, "We are more than conquerors through him who loved us" (Rom. 8:37 ESV).

The apostles advise us to look more deeply into the source of our everyday struggles, temptations, and trials. In nearly every situation, our primary problems either arise from our hearts or are sent to expose what's in us, so we can change by God's grace. Nevertheless, we also have an enemy who seeks our harm and hinders the witness of Christ's church. From the highest heights of the angelic realm to the deepest depths of our hearts, darkness lurks ready to create havoc in the world and erupt in violence.

ARMED AND DANGEROUS

My brother served in the Navy Special Forces and now has a business that makes defensive gear for SWAT Teams, the military, and embassies around the world. Furnishing the warriors who protect the peace is a critical job and he takes his work seriously. His mission statement is simple: "Equipping Warriors in Harm's Way." That's exactly what Paul is doing in Ephesians 6:10–18. If Paul worked for my brother, he'd be sending out large crates of "the armor of God" and equipping every Christian for conflict.

This is a little book, so we don't have space to take a deep dive into all the armor Paul lists. It's important to see, however, that he calls it "the armor of God" rather than *our* armor.[1] Some commentators suggest that Paul based his thoughts on the Roman soldiers with whom he was—sadly—far

---

1   For a more comprehensive look at "the armor of God," consider reading William Gurnall's, *The Christian in Complete Armor.*

too familiar. They suggest he saw in their gear an excellent image of a Christian ready for the fight. But I don't think that's right at all.

Instead, Paul draws on Isaiah. There, the Lord says he will put on his armor and fight for his people:

> [The Lord] saw that there was no man,
>   and wondered that there was no one to intercede;
> then his own arm brought him salvation,
>   and his righteousness upheld him.
> He put on righteousness as a breastplate,
>   and a helmet of salvation on his head;
> he put on garments of vengeance for clothing,
>   and wrapped himself in zeal as a cloak.
> (Isa. 59:16–17 ESV; see parallels in Eph. 6:14, 17)

Isaiah 52:7 also says, "How lovely on the mountains are the feet of those who bring good news (gospel), announcing peace, proclaiming news of happiness, saying, 'Our God reigns!'" Our sandals are the Birkenstocks of Jesus, who brings the glad tidings of God's kingdom to his people and in so doing drives out the dark powers (see Eph. 6:15).

Paul's main point is that our victory over the devil in "the evil day" is rooted in Christ's own victory over Satan. His victory is now ours. We fight by "standing," a stationary position that immediately reminds us of Moses' words to Israel when they were pursued by the Egyptian army and on the cusp of disaster at the Red Sea: "Do not fear! Stand by and see the salvation of the Lord" (Exod. 14:13). We don't triumph over the darkness by flailing about wildly with our weapons but by resolutely standing on God's promise to deliver us. We trust in his power rather than in our own.

POINTS OF ATTACK

What sorts of attacks does Satan mount against Christ's church? What are his objectives, and how can we best prepare for his assaults? Let's briefly note six "fiery missiles" the enemy launches and then three key responses we must make in the face of these attacks.[2]

1. Temptation

Sin is deceitful (Heb. 3:13) and so is the human heart: It is "more deceitful than all else" (Jer. 17:9). So our hearts, by which we lie to ourselves and others, are the perfect match for sin, which deceptively offers to satisfy our heart's desires. That's why James wrote, "But each person is tempted when he is lured and enticed by his own desire. Then desire when it has conceived gives birth to sin, and sin, when it is fully grown, brings forth death" (James 1:14–15 ESV). Temptations are an inside-out game. Our hearts are seduced by whatever shiny objects present themselves, disguised by the enemy as offers of power, prestige, and pleasure.

Satan, a limited being, isn't tempting every single Christian all the time. As James makes clear, temptations arise from our disordered desires, which take legitimate gifts of God and make them objects of our supreme desire in place of God. We don't go looking for a demon behind every door or, if we succumb to temptation, relieve ourselves of responsibility by claiming, "The devil made me do it." Galatians makes clear that everything from immorality to outbursts of anger find their origin in our "flesh," not in demons sent to harass us. Even sorcery is a "deed of the flesh" rather than a dark art inspired by Satan (Gal. 5:19–21).

---

2   One note by way of reminder: Our primary problems either originate with us, arising from our hearts, or they're sent to expose what's in us so we can change by God's grace. A great deal of the devil's work is simply to push the buttons of the sin we nourish within.

We also need to distinguish between what we're tempted *by* and what we're tempted *to*. I may be tempted *by* the wealth or beauty of another, but this means I'm being tempted *to* envy, lust, or greed—issues arising in my heart. Their wealth or beauty is not necessarily sinful, but my attitude towards them may be utterly sinful. Satan presents to us the perfectly permissible in order to draw out the illicit loves and passions we harbor within (see Mark 7:21–23). We tend to blame the exterior attraction without adequately dealing with our interior twistedness. We believe the lie that this new toy will finally make our hearts be quiet, sated, and full at last. It's not the position, person, or the possession that's sinful but the posture of our hearts. Have we opened the door for the lie that "taking and eating" the treat will do the trick? The legalist despises the external and shames it—*Look at the way they dress! Look at that wastefulness!*—always blaming sin on another. But the Christian who knows God's grace doesn't look upon God's gifts as sinful in themselves. Instead, he deals with the law of sin within, seeking God's mercy to transform his heart. There's nothing sinful about a Ferrari, but if I look at it with covetousness or envy its owner, I'm giving into the sin that arises in my heart.

We can also be tempted by pain to despair. The gnawing, persistent presence within us of certain temptations can lead us into deep bouts of doubt, self-loathing, anger, and even walking away from the faith. If Satan can't get us to give up the faith for pleasure, he may well seek to induce us to give it up in response to psychological, spiritual, or physical pain. Our recourse is, as always, the cross of Christ, where we enter into "the fellowship of His sufferings" (Phil. 3:10). When we do this, hell's powers are shaken to their very foundations. As the senior demon Screwtape writes to his protégé in C.S. Lewis' work, *The Screwtape Letters*, "Do not be deceived, Wormwood. Our cause is never more in danger than when a human, no longer desiring, but still intending, to do our Enemy's will, looks round upon a universe from which every trace of Him seems to have vanished, and asks why he has been forsaken, and still obeys."[3]

In a similar way, we can find ourselves tempted to *not* do what's right when it must be done. What lies are at work in our hearts at this point of attack? They are legion. Perhaps we imagine that taking action or speaking up will prove too costly. We might lose friends, influence, social standing, or a job. In the most extreme circumstances, we might lose our lives. We're tempted *by* our pride *to* avoid conflict, embarrassment, or loss. We're tempted *by* our fear *to* withhold generous giving which would expand the kingdom and alleviate the suffering of others. These sins arise from within, too—our pleasures and comforts seem more valuable than Christ and his reproach.

When tempted, we do well to recall our Savior's victory over the temptations presented to him (see Matthew 4 and Luke 4 for accounts of these encounters with Satan). Despite his hunger after forty days without food, Christ refused to turn stones into bread; he was the only stone that could become bread for the world. He refused to accept authority over all the kingdoms of the world by bowing his knee to Satan; all the kingdoms were already his as God's king. He refused to prove he was God's Son by hurling himself from the pinnacle of the Temple to be rescued by holy angels; the fact that the temptation was offered was all the proof that was needed. In every way, our Lord reversed the fall of Adam, refusing the lust of the flesh, the lust of the eyes, and the pride of life, securing our ultimate triumph over the tempter by his own victory. Just as Adam's rebellion had sealed the doom of humanity, so the second Adam's obedience has sealed our redemption. It's through Jesus' triumph in the face of evil that the Christian is rescued from the snare of Satan.[4]

---

3 C.S. Lewis, *The Screwtape Letters* (London: The Centenary Press, 1942), 47. I know of no more incisive and entertaining volume about Satan's infernal strategies than Lewis's masterful work set in World War II London. If you've not yet read it, I hope you will.

4 For a remarkable treatment of the way Satan uses temptation to strike at us and how we may resist him,

2. Accusation

Satan is referred to as "the accuser of our brothers" (Rev. 12:9–10 ESV) and this tactic moves in four directions.[5] First, Satan seeks to bring accusations against a Christian before God's tribunal. But any accusation would be quickly dismissed because Christ bore the Christian's guilt on the cross and fully paid the penalty for that sin. The Christian stands before God with the righteousness of Christ imputed to him by grace alone and received by faith alone. We'd really be in a perilous situation if we attempted to justify ourselves before God on the basis of our own righteousness. But since we stand in Christ's perfect righteousness, we can rest assured that no accusation made against us in heaven can prevail. This is why Paul wrote, "Who shall bring any charge against God's elect? It is God who justifies. Who is to condemn? Christ Jesus is the one who died—more than that, who was raised—who is at the right hand of God, who indeed is interceding for us" (Rom. 8:33–34 ESV).

Here are three key truths about potential accusations made against us, whether in heaven or in our hearts (see 1 John 1:9–10; 2:1–2):

> » First, if we think there's nothing sinful about us, we're self-deluded. Yes, we're justified by faith alone through grace alone, but we're also still sinful and it's essential for us to say so, to confess our sins to God.

---

please read Thomas Brooks' *Precious Remedies Against Satan's Devices* (Feather Trail Press, 2010). I know of no other book like it, offering insight into the way the tempter works, especially his lies about sin, and the remedies available to us as we may strengthened for our struggle against his advances.

5   We need to make an important qualification here. It is *not* Satan's activity when people make valid charges against people who have abused others, whether in the workplace or in the church. Regulations in those spheres determine what constitutes abuse and how such charges are to be handled, and we urge all to follow those to the letter. This is especially incumbent on church leaders when they encounter such accusations. Abuse victims frequently suffer from fear and shame and only very reluctantly bring such charges against a superior or spiritual leader. The accuser has a responsibility to be truthful and accurate, presenting appropriate witnesses and evidence, and those who hear the accusation have a great responsibility to handle the victim of alleged abuse with compassion, understanding, and decisive action in accordance with civil laws and institutional policies.

» When we confess our sins to God, he forgives and cleanses us of all sin, completely and totally. Why? It's not because we've met his requirements but because we've acknowledged that we haven't and can't—and that Christ has done so on our behalf.

» All charges against us are baseless because our advocate with the Father is our savior Jesus, who intercedes for us. His blood is the propitiation—the atonement—for our sins and completely removes the stain of our sin.

We also see Satan whisper accusations in our hearts against one another in the church. Subtle but baseless lies distort friendships and ruin fellowship. I'm sure you can think of a thousand examples of these sinister thoughts that creep into our imaginations about our friends; they need to be immediately dismissed, followed by actions taken to prove their falsehood. Remember that people are often going through all kinds of struggles, and their conduct on a particular day typically has very little to do with us.

Satan can also accuse us to ourselves. He happily drags out our past failures—they are many!—but we must remember these as *forgiven* sins. Our remembrance of Christ's death at the Lord's Table is the answer to the memories our enemy would have us dwell on. He'll point us to our sins, but we must immediately point him to the cross. In fact, I often agree with the devil on his charges about my past sins: *Yes, you're right. I did that. But do you see the cross over there? Do you see my Savior and his blood? Yes! You do! He's my righteousness! Be gone!* John is once again helpful here. He writes, "if our heart condemns us … God is greater than our heart, and He knows all things" (1 John 3:20).

Lastly, Satan will animate certain persons and powers in the culture to make accusations against the church in an effort to discredit her witness.

This has been the case since the very beginning. While we should always seek to humbly and respectfully offer the church's reason for hope and defend her against falsehood, these attacks are an opportunity to return good for evil, turn the other cheek, and allow our deeds of love and service to speak for themselves. Peter wrote:

> Keep your conduct among the Gentiles honorable, so that when they speak against you as evildoers, they may see your good deeds and glorify God on the day of visitation …. For this is the will of God, that by doing good you should put to silence the ignorance of foolish people. (1 Pet. 2:12, 15 ESV)

3. Division

We learned at the outset that one meaning of the word *devil* is *divider*, and Satan has sought to divide churches, families, and friends since the beginning. Jesus prays for the visible unity of his church as a witness in the world (John 17:21), and Paul exhorts the churches he served to "keep the unity of the Spirit in the bond of peace" (Eph. 4:3), and to be of "the same mind … intent on one purpose" (Phil. 2:1ff). God commands his blessing where his people are unified before him (Ps. 133), so it's no surprise that Satan will always seek to divide us from one another.

This means we must diligently work for reconciliation between Christians estranged from one another, as Paul did with two women who were his co-workers in the gospel (Phil. 4:2–3). While there are times when divisions in the church are necessary because of infidelity to the truth of the gospel, many of our divisions are motivated by politics, social standing, race, and unresolved conflicts. None of these should define the boundaries of our fellowship. The divider delights to highlight our differences and sins against one another. But Jesus said, "Blessed are the peacemakers," and we must be such servants in these divisive days.

4. Deception

Jesus said that Satan is "a liar and the father of all lies" (John 8:44). Most Christians are aware that the devil seeks to blind the minds of the unbelieving to the truth of the gospel and mislead the church through false teaching and leaders. Paul steadfastly warned the churches against this possibility and fiercely intervened when this danger was being realized. Discussing false apostles, Paul wrote that we shouldn't be surprised when they're present since "even Satan disguises himself as an angel of light" (2 Cor. 11:14). We must be rooted and grounded in God's love, established in the truth of the gospel, and steadfast in the faith. The truth of Jesus and his gospel isn't a trampoline one can bounce around on; it's a solid wall to protect us and an unshakable, unchangeable foundation for our lives that we can count on, now and in eternity.

That's why Paul warned the Galatians about false teachers and fake news gospels in such strident terms: "There are some who are disturbing you and want to distort the gospel of Christ," he wrote, "But even if we, or an angel from heaven, should preach to you a gospel contrary to the one we preached to you, he is to be accursed! As we have said before, even now I say again: If anyone is preaching to you a gospel contrary to what you received, he is to be accursed" (Gal. 1:7–9). There are many issues on which Christians can grant one another great latitude and liberty, pursuing unity with a posture of charity. But when it comes to the gospel, no compromise can be permitted. We must contend for the "faith once and for all delivered" to the church (Jude 3). This is the only way to avoid the poison offered by false teachers—those who teach falsely and those who live falsely, those who deny the truth and those who discredit the truth.

There are numerous other forms of spiritual deception, of course. If we listen to God's word but don't act on it, we can deceive ourselves with false piety (James 1:22). We can imagine that we have risen to lofty spiritual heights of maturity and giftedness when in fact we still have plenty of room to grow (Rom. 12:3). New Age spiritualism, occult practices, atheism, pantheism, and the wildly divergent spiritist religions of tribal Africa all present deceptive beliefs about God, humanity, and the way of salvation. Despite the presence of beauty, wisdom, and truth in Hinduism, Sikhism, Buddhism, and Islam, these systems cannot provide the light needed to know God and receive the gift of eternal life. They either deny the truth about Jesus as he is revealed in Scripture or promote ancient forms of idolatry as alternative paths to salvation.

5. Enslavement

Whether caught in a prison of resentment or addiction, many people find themselves trapped by Satan's work, unable to escape the clutches of his power. Paul encouraged Timothy to help those who were bound to "come to their senses and escape from the snare of the devil, having been held captive by him to do his will" (2 Tim. 2:26). The word for *capture* is a military term used for prisoners of war. Repeated sinful activity can result in habits from which it's difficult to break free. This doesn't mean that those so entrapped have ceased to be true Christians, but we need God's grace to break into the prisons that hold these captives and liberate them from their chains. This grace is given in God's word and by his Spirit through ministries in the church and sometimes through medical and psychological counsel.

Jesus said, "If you continue in my word, then you are truly my disciples; and you will know the truth, and the truth will set you free" (John 8:31–32). When we confess our need for the freedom he alone can give, we encounter Jesus' liberating presence through his word, which can free us forever from all that holds us captive.

6. Suffering

All human beings suffer, and Christians are not spared this. Paul wrote frequently of his experiences, which included terrible physical pain and mental anguish. This suffering was often a result of his mission—Jesus told Paul he was called to suffer (Acts 9:16), and he was often imprisoned and beaten. His life was threatened (see 2 Cor. 11:16–12:10 for Paul's review of his many ordeals). He viewed his painful experiences as an opportunity to grow closer to Jesus Christ, entering "the fellowship of his sufferings" (Phil. 3:7–14). Paul knew the experiences of being falsely accused, having his work and reputation undermined, and the loneliness and betrayal of being abandoned by cherished friends. In the end, Paul was likely martyred for his faith in Jesus, executed by command of the Roman Emperor.

While Paul saw these sufferings as part of his calling, he also recognized Satan's hand in at least some of them. He called his 'thorn in the flesh' a "messenger of Satan to torment me" (2 Cor. 12:7). While Scripture isn't clear about precisely what the thorn might've been, we do know a few key things that help us understand suffering. First, we know its origin—Satan. Secondly, we know that Paul had an odd view of it. While it was sent from Satan, it was also a gift given to him that had a positive impact on his personal holiness. Finally, we can also see that God was glorified in this suffering. God didn't deliver Paul from that thorn but instead gave him the grace to endure it. He used it to bring Paul to a place of weakness in which God's power could shine through his life:

> Three times I pleaded with the Lord about this, that it should leave me. But he said to me, "My grace is sufficient for you, for my power is made perfect in weakness." Therefore I will boast all the more gladly of my weaknesses, so that the power of Christ may rest upon me. For the sake of Christ, then, I am content with weaknesses, insults, hardships, persecutions, and calamities. For when I am weak, then I am strong. (2 Cor. 12:8–10 ESV)

Satan's hope in our suffering is to cause our souls to shrivel to the point of denying our faith. But God's design for our suffering is to strengthen our souls to depend on his power and demonstrate the faith. Whether suffering takes the form of persistent temptation, disease, death, grief, persecution, mental illness, sins, deep and perpetual loneliness, or even crimes committed against us, every life is visited by suffering in some measure. Satan has succeeded in using this problem of pain to ruin the faith of some people who can't reconcile how a good God would allow so much suffering in the world.

Whether the issue is a pandemic or persecution, children abandoning the faith or an infant who dies, all suffering can either threaten or strengthen our faith. In pain, we turn to the savior who's our example in suffering. With him, we can find the solace we need in our sorrows, the place to weep with him who wept at the tomb of his friend, and the hope we must have in order to endure what's yet before us. Together we confess that Christ not only suffered for us as our substitute but left us "an example for us to follow in his steps" (1 Pet. 2:21).

THREE WAYS WE RESIST THE ENEMY

In the face of such terrible assaults on our faith, how can we "resist the devil" so that he will "flee" from us (James 4:7)?

1. We must rest in Christ's victory over the enemy.

We can sing in the storm because we know that Christ has won the battle. When Cuban Christians were being executed in the early days of Castro's Marxist regime, they went to their death singing, *Viva Cristo Rey!* (*Long Live Christ the King!*). How can people sing in the face of death? By resting in the death and resurrection of Jesus.

As we fight, we don't win every battle. It's a long war to drive the usurper from the territory that Christ won through his death and resurrection. The ultimate outcome is certain, but as we move towards that great final day, we'll experience attacks and setbacks. We'll fail at times and must be quick to repent and repair the damage we've done. We may find that our faith is sometimes very weak, and we might wish that it were stronger. But we have a savior who couldn't be more powerful. If we're his, it's not because our trust never wavers, but because his love never fails.

2. We must learn to stand on Christ's word.

Take up "the sword of the Spirit, which is the word of God," wrote Paul (Eph. 6:17). When Christ pushed back Satan's temptations in the wilderness, he did so by quoting Scripture, specifically Deuteronomy, the book of Israel's history in the wilderness. Christ in the wilderness, living out Israel's forty-year sojourn over the course of forty days, took the word of God from that past experience and made it his own for the wilderness temptations he faced. We must do the same. The wilderness of temptation and testing is unavoidable and is set between the promise of a new land and its inheritance. For every Christian, between the promise made and the fulfillment realized, there's a problem to conquer, and it can only be done by standing on God's word. We live by the Scriptures, saying to Jesus with Peter, "Lord, to whom shall we go? You have the words of eternal life" (John 6:68).

We live by faith in God's word, revealed to his apostles and recorded in the Scriptures. We can't resist the enemy in our own power, but instead rely on Christ's; we have victory not by our own cleverness but by God's unchanging truth. Nor do we usually do this on our own. Our stand is taken side-by-side and arm-in-arm with other brothers and sisters in the church. We may face a terrible personal trial, but we can better persevere in it and battle against it with the aid of our band of brothers and sisters who fight alongside us.

3. We must look for Christ's return.

Our enemy is indeed a terrible foe. He may even prevail against us at times, just as for a brief moment he prevailed over Christ and saw to his death. But in the end, he'll be utterly cast out and thrown into the Lake of Fire (Rev. 20). Just as Jesus saw Satan "fall from heaven like lightning," so we too shall also soon see "Satan crushed beneath [our] feet" (Rom. 16:20). Faced with the limits of our understanding, wrestling with the "law of sin" within, and pushing back against the night in which we often find ourselves, we must trust God. While he may not remove the thorn that afflicts us, he will be glorified in our weakness and soon turn our mourning into dancing. Do we have a frightening lion bearing down upon us? We might feel ourselves in the grip of his terrible jaws! Yet even in death we will confess with Paul, "I was rescued out of the lion's mouth. The Lord will rescue me from every evil deed, and will bring me safely into His heavenly kingdom. To Him be the glory forever and ever. Amen" (2 Tim. 4:17–18).

"The God of peace will soon crush Satan
under your feet."

Romans 16:20

CHAPTER FOUR

FAQs on the Devil and His Work

ARE EXORCISMS STILL NECESSARY AND ARE THE
CLAIMS MADE ABOUT THEM VALID? ISN'T IT TRUE
THAT WHAT PEOPLE USED TO CALL "DEMONS" WE NOW
KNOW TO BE MENTAL ILLNESSES AND WE TREAT THEM
ACCORDINGLY?

An exorcism is a religious rite in which a demon that has physically and psychically possessed a person is driven out. In the Roman Catholic tradition, such exorcisms are conducted by a certified church leader or team through the invocation of the name of Jesus and the authority of the church. Most conservative Catholic, Orthodox, and Protestant Christians agree that demons are real entities and that they can sometimes so control someone that the person is said to be possessed. When that occurs an exorcism is sometimes believed to be necessary to liberate the person from the demon's grip.

When possessed, a person loses control of his body and mental faculties and manifests unusual phenomena, such as speaking in foreign languages or different voices, remarkable physical strength, insight into the lives of those performing the exorcism, and levitation. All of this suggests that the personality of the demon has eclipsed the mind and will of the victim. Such extreme behavior is sometimes judged to be demonic rather than a mental illness, but only after strict examination guidelines have been followed in order to determine the mental and physical health of the person thought to be possessed. Christians in Europe and North America rightly view with suspicion claims that all such manifestations are demonic and therefore look first to other potential causes of unusual behavior. In many Asian, African, and Latin American cultures, such examinations are often held to be unnecessary because demonic manifestations are not viewed as unusual. Such possessions are reported frequently by missionaries in these regions, where spiritist religions and occult activity are common.

Where such religions are practiced in the West, one can expect to see dark powers exerting levels of influence most would find highly unusual and even dramatic. The examples of demon possession in the Gospels and Acts are frequently violent and terrifying, and no one should take lightly the power of such entities where they are indeed truly at work.[1]

CAN A CHRISTIAN BE DEMON-POSSESSED?

If by possession one means utter control and enslavement, the answer is no. This doesn't mean that a Christian can't be influenced by dark forces or attacked by them. When Peter sought to stop Jesus from going to Jerusalem, Jesus rebuked him saying, "Get behind me, Satan! You are a stumbling block to me" (Matt. 16:23). Peter was not possessed, but he certainly was influenced by Satan without being aware of it.

Many ancient Christian baptismal rites include the question, "Do you renounce the devil, all of his works, and all of his ways?" This means that baptism was understood as a kind of exorcism, liberating the baptized

---

1   Acts 19 records a cautionary tale for all who presumptuously set about doing exorcisms. When a group of Jewish exorcists sought to cast out a demon "in the name of Jesus whom Paul preaches," the demon not only refused to comply with their eviction order but responded, "Jesus I know and Paul I know, but who are you?" before setting upon them and leaving them badly injured. In Luke 11, Jesus appears to give a blanket commission to all his followers to drive out demons, but his words, "I have given you authority to tread upon serpents and scorpions and over all the power of the enemy, and nothing shall in any way harm you" is part of a temporary and limited commission to a particular group of disciples. Making it a license for any believer to begin a "deliverance ministry" is an unwise and misleading view of the text.

from the dark powers that would seek to pursue them and drag them back into slavery. Our baptisms into the name of Jesus are an essential deliverance from the clutches of Satan and into the gracious and strong hands of the Almighty.

This doesn't mean that everyone who professes to be a Christian is free from the possibility of possession. The professing Christian couple Ananias and Sapphira lied to the Holy Spirit at the cost of their lives, an action that was a result of Satan filling their hearts (Acts 5:3). They weren't manifesting the presence of demons in the way people might normally expect, but their high-handed deception showed a possession had taken place. Many mental health workers can tell you tales of those suffering from various forms of religious mania who claim to be Christians but also at times claim to be prophets or apostles or even the Messiah. On some occasions, these situations may warrant the description of "possession." Some who name Christ have engaged in murder or other acts of violence, sometimes defending their actions by claiming that they'd heard God tell them to commit the crime. We also note the case of Simon the Sorcerer who, despite having professed faith, was caught in the web of Satanic darkness (Acts 8:13, 18–23). Someone who professes the faith doesn't necessarily possess the faith. On some occasions, those who profess faith become the possessed, as was the case with Judas Iscariot.

Christians are warned about being impacted by "deceitful spirits and teachings of demons" (1 Tim. 4:1). We also note that a woman who was a "daughter of Abraham" and suffering from a physical condition that left her bent over and unable to straighten up was "bound" by Satan for "eighteen long years" and ought to be freed, a miraculous liberation which Jesus immediately performed (Luke 13:11). In other parts of this booklet, we've noted Satan's strategies to delay, derail, and deceive us. Paul was concerned about his beloved Corinthian Christians being led astray by the devil's efforts to deceive them (2 Cor. 11:3). We must be on the alert against him, but we cannot be possessed by him or his agents.

WHO OR WHAT WERE THE NEPHILIM? DID FALLEN ANGELS INTERMARRY WITH HUMAN WOMEN TO PRODUCE A RACE OF GIANTS?

This is a subject of considerable debate among scholars. Genesis refers to "the sons of God" who intermarry with the daughters of men and produce the Nephilim, a race of giants. This episode occurs as an example of the horror into which humankind has been plunged by sin and as a prelude to God's judgement on the world through the flood (Gen. 6:1–8). Noting that the phrase "sons of God" is used elsewhere in the Scriptures to describe a heavenly council meeting of angelic beings before God's throne, many conclude that these beings are some of the fallen angels (Job 1:6; 2:1; 38:7; Ps. 82:1; 89:6; 1 Kings 22:19–23). Ancient Jewish literature like *1 Enoch* and many early church fathers certainly take that view, and it's possible that this is what Peter is referring to when he writes that Christ "also went and made proclamation to the spirits in prison, who once were disobedient when the patience of God kept waiting in the days of Noah, during the construction of the ark, in which a few, that is, eight persons, were brought safely through the water" (1 Pet. 3:19–20). The further references to this episode in 2 Peter and Jude, both of which draw on *1 Enoch*, may also support this view. Peter describes a time when "God did not spare angels when they sinned, but cast them into hell and committed them to pits of darkness, held for judgment; and did not spare the ancient world, but protected Noah, a preacher of righteousness, with seven others, when He brought a flood upon the world of the ungodly" (2 Pet. 2:4–5).

Noting that in the resurrection we do not marry but "are as the angels"

(Matt. 22:30), other scholars hold that Genesis can't refer to angels because angels can't engage in sexual union. In that case, "sons of God" refers not to angels but to the descendants of Seth, the son of Adam and Eve, through whom the line of promise is established that leads to the birth of the Messiah. The horror of Genesis 6 was that the holy line was endangered by Sethites marrying "the daughters of men" outside the covenant of promise.

Another view suggests that the Nephilim are military warriors, and the "sons of God" are Ancient Near Eastern kings gathering harems. [2] All sides of the discussion have their proponents and are not without their problems.[3]

ARE GHOSTS REAL? ARE THEY REALLY THE DEAD WHO HAVE NOT YET MOVED ON TO THEIR ETERNAL DESTINATION?

Most claims of phantoms and ghost sightings are fraudulent. The appearance of the *Cottingley Fairies* is one noteworthy example.[4] It captured the whole of Britain, but years later the sisters who claimed to have seen these fairies confessed that it was a joke.

According to the Bible, the soul departs from the body at death and goes immediately to its destination where it awaits Judgement Day. For the Christian, to be absent from the body is to be present with the

---

2   See David VanDrunen, *Politics After Christendom: Political Theology in a Fractured World* (Grand Rapids, MI: Zondervan, 2020), 335.

3   For another detailed discussion of these issues and passages, see Michael Heiser, *The Unseen Realm* (Bellingham, Washington, Lexham Press), p. 92–109. For the Sethite view, see Sydney H.T. Page, *Powers of Evil: A Biblical Study of Satan & Demons* (Grand Rapids, Michigan, Baker Book House, 1995), 43–54. See also Rita Cefalu, "Royal Priestly Heirs to the Restoration Promise of Genesis 3:15: A Biblical Theological Perspective on the Sons of God in Genesis 6." *Westminster Theological Journal 76*, no 2 (2014), 351–370.

4   https://www.historic-uk.com/CultureUK/The-Fairies-of-Cottingley/

Lord, awaiting vindication. The unbeliever is also immediately separated from the body, but tragically so. Scripture is clear: "It is destined for people to die once, and after this comes judgment" (Heb. 9:27). I enjoy a good ghost story as much as anyone. I especially delight in Charles Dickens' *A Christmas Carol*, in which the late Jacob Marley appears in shackles and chains to Scrooge, dropping by while wandering the earth in penitence. According to Scripture, though, no such wandering about is going on and no second chances are being handed out to the dead. "Marley was dead, to begin with," Dickens writes. Biblically speaking, that was that for Marley.

In my view, any supernatural appearances claiming to be ghosts of the deceased are in fact what the Scriptures call "familiar spirits," demons that impersonate the dead in order to seduce the grieving into the clutches of darkness. Yes, the witch of Endor did summon Samuel from the grave to have a word with King Saul (1 Sam. 28), but that was not the normal course of things. Moses appears on the Mount of Transfiguration with Elijah and Jesus, but not as a "ghost," and the same is true of the resurrected saints walking about the streets of Jerusalem on the first Easter morning (Matt. 27:52). These were not ghosts haunting the city, but saints freed from the realm of the dead by Christ's resurrection victory and headed to heaven. We should not expect to see the departed until the great moment when we are reunited in glory, and we should dismiss all other sightings either as a magician's trick or a devilish deception. In either case, we can ignore them.

DOES THE DEVIL KNOW MY THOUGHTS?

Sometimes I think my smartphone can read my thoughts, but when it comes to the devil, the answer is generally no. This question might have something to do with the fact that people sometimes see Satan as a kind of equal combatant with God himself. But Satan is not omniscient, omnipresent, or omnipotent. He's a creature made by the Creator and, while powerful, he's also limited. I have little doubt that dark powers have a decent dossier on hand to keep them up to date on what works to tempt us, but unless God were to somehow give them permission to know our thoughts, the devils are not privy to our interior life.

Many Christian leaders have written that the devils are set on putting thoughts into our minds (Augustine, Lombard, Aquinas, and many others), and that's not so hard to imagine. The serpent started the conversation with Eve and led her into temptation by making suggestions to her about God's character and word that led her to reconsider his goodness and the wisdom of forbidding such delicious fruit to her and her husband. So while the enemy isn't reading our thoughts, he will try to plant evil thoughts in us that would lead us astray.

IS IT OK FOR CHRISTIANS TO READ HOROSCOPES OR PARTICIPATE IN FORTUNE-TELLING?

I know many people regard such things as harmless fun and, left to that, they might simply be entertaining and good for a laugh. They could be regarded as no more harmful than reading a prediction from a fortune cookie. Yet many people take such things seriously and build their lives around the guidance that the stars and the tarot offer them. Trusting in the stars to guide our lives or looking to occult powers for help is forbidden in the Scriptures. Here are just a few examples:

> » "There shall not be found among you anyone who burns his son or his daughter as an offering, anyone who practices divination or tells fortunes or interprets omens, or a sorcerer or a charmer or a medium or a necromancer or one who inquires of the dead, for

whoever does these things is an abomination to the Lord. And because of these abominations the Lord your God is driving them out before you. You shall be blameless before the Lord your God, for these nations, which you are about to dispossess, listen to fortune-tellers and to diviners. But as for you, the Lord your God has not allowed you to do this. The Lord your God will raise up for you a prophet like me from among you, from your brothers—it is to him you shall listen." (Deut. 18:10–15).

» "Let your astrologers come forward, those stargazers who make predictions month by month, let them save you from what is coming upon you" (Isa. 47:13).

» "But for the cowardly, and unbelieving, and abominable, and murderers, and sexually immoral persons, and sorcerers, and idolaters, and all liars, their part will be in the lake that burns with fire and brimstone, which is the second death" (Rev. 21:8).

Scripture is clear that these practices belong to people who don't know God and that we must avoid them. Christians must not look to other spiritual forces for guidance when we have Christ, his word, and his Spirit to guide our lives. We listen to and follow Jesus Christ.

DOES PLAYING WITH AN OUIJA BOARD OPEN YOUR SOUL UP TO SATAN?

This question is related to the one we've just examined. Christians should avoid attempts to communicate with the dead or look for guidance from a spirit other than the Holy Spirit. Can this well-known board game become a portal for demons to enter our lives? That was the storyline in *The Exorcist*, a really scary book that became a classic horror film.

The truth is that it isn't the board game but the heart's openness to a lying spirit that is the portal for darkness. Innocent play doesn't lead to demon possession. But use resulting from a desire for a forbidden look into the unseen realm can invite to the door of our lives entities that will seek to entrap and destroy souls.

IS IT OKAY FOR CHRISTIANS TO CELEBRATE HALLOWEEN?

Halloween is a word that's derived from the Old English *All Hallows Eve*, the night before All Saints Day. The Feast of All Saints, celebrated on November 1, is a day on many church calendars that commemorates the martyrs and great Christian leaders whose names we don't know. You're no doubt familiar with St. Patrick's Day or St. Valentine's Day, and might even be familiar with St. Nicholas' Day. All Saints Day caught all the saints we might overlook. The day before, October 31, was "All Hallows Eve," just as December 24 is Christmas Eve.

The Protestant Reformers pointed out that endless saints' days were a terrible burden and stopped marking them because they weren't required by Scripture. It was fine if you wanted to mark it, but it was wrong if a church required it.

Those who had always observed All Hallows Eve were celebrating the defeat of the devil and death by the great heroes of the faith. Like all celebrations, it could all get a bit sideways and in Britain, some of the old Celtic Druid customs were added in.

I'm with the Reformers on this one, neither requiring nor forbidding it. We're free people and can't have our consciences bound to mark certain days as holy when the New Testament doesn't require that.

But there's nothing necessarily wrong with celebrating that death and Satan are defeated. If we want to, we can throw parties to celebrate great victories over terrible foes. That's the way I view All Hallows Eve! Pass the candy.[5]

I especially recall that Martin Luther chose October 31 to nail up his ninety-five theses on the Wittenberg Church door. He was going after the false views of purgatory and outlining our freedom in the gospel. Like Luther, our consciences are bound to the word of God, and this is a conscience issue for the Christian. You're free to celebrate the defeat of Satan or, if it appears too close to paganism for comfort, you're free to pass it by.

SOMETIMES I HEAR PEOPLE SAY THEY "BIND THE DEVIL" WHEN THEY PRAY. IS THAT SOMETHING WE CAN DO? IS THAT A GOOD WAY TO PRAY?

It's never a good idea to get into a conversation with the devil. These notions come from two sources. First, they arise from some peculiar but popular views on spiritual warfare that claim we need to discover the primary demonic stronghold over an area and then "bind it" to stop its influence. Second, the language of binding is used by Jesus to describe what he does to Satan as he conquers him and rescues people from his power (Matt. 12:29). Revelation also shows Satan being "bound," but in this case, it's by a strong angel (Rev. 20:1–3).

In neither case do we bind Satan! We do drive him out through the

---

5   That doesn't mean one embraces or endorses whatever may pass as a Halloween celebration. Lawlessness, drunkenness, and immorality in its all of its varied forms are always sinful, no matter the situation or occasion.

preaching of the gospel, but this is because he's already bound by Christ and his holy angels. We don't command Satan about. As Jude said, even the Archangel Michael was careful with the words he used when he defeated Satan in a battle over the body of Moses: "But when the archangel Michael, contending with the devil, was disputing about the body of Moses, he did not presume to pronounce a blasphemous judgment, but said, "The Lord rebuke you" (Jude 10). Don't speak to the devil, whether in prayer or elsewhere!

HOW CAN I TELL IF MY SUFFERING IS AN ATTACK FROM SATAN THAT I SHOULD RESIST OR A TRIAL GOD IS TAKING ME THROUGH FOR MY GOOD?

I don't think the answer to this question is always easily evident. We've looked at Paul's thorn as an example of this. We don't know exactly what that thorn was, but Paul wrote that it was a messenger sent to him from Satan. Yet when he prayed, God did not deliver him, allowing this thorn to be a source of sanctification in Paul's life. Paul said the thorn kept him from the pride that could have arisen because of the remarkable visions of God's glory that had been entrusted to him. What an irony. The work of Satan, the most prideful being in history, served to deliver Paul from the pride which might have caused him to stumble (2 Cor. 12).

So even if we know something is from Satan, that doesn't mean we will be immediately delivered from it. It's also true that if handled humbly, our suffering may cause us to grow in grace. Ultimately the attack of Satan, which God clearly permits, leads to the defeat of Satan in our lives and in the church. We can't always understand why God permits terrible suffering in our lives, but we can trust him to strengthen us in these ordeals and use them for our good and his glory.

DO WE EACH HAVE A GUARDIAN ANGEL?

In *City of God,* Augustine wrote, "I hope to demonstrate that there is no absurdity . . . in asserting a fellowship between men and angels."[6] He certainly did his level best with that project, writing at length about the holy angels and our shared fellowship, especially in worship. The line between humans and angels is dotted, and they pass back and forth between our realm and theirs. But even the great Augustine had to admit that we "know not altogether what angels are."

We could use an entire book on angels, but as we've already noted, they're spiritual entities created by God that are described as "winds" and "flames." They're fierce warriors when they need to be, help one another when under duress from opposing forces, and talk with one another about what is happening with people. Some are designated as "princes" and others as "watchers" (Dan. 4:13; 10:21). Jesus said that our care for children is augmented by the fact that "their angels" see God's face (Matt. 18:10). We read that "the angel of the Lord encamps around those who fear him to deliver them" (Ps. 34:7), and Psalm 91 speaks of the angels as our protectors. Hebrews also notes that they are "ministering spirits sent out to serve the heirs of salvation" (Heb. 1:14). Certain angels were entrusted with the guardianship of nations and peoples (Dan. 2, 9–10), the deliverance of individuals, and the execution of fiery judgments on entire cities (Gen. 19:1–25). The Lord told Moses, "Behold, I send my angel before you, to keep you, and to bring you into the place which I have prepared" (Exod. 23:20). It's safe to say that Joel Miller is right: "The demons desire our demise, but the angels take wing in our defense."[7]

---

6   Saint Augustine, *City of God* (United Kingdom: Penguin Books Limited, 2003), Book XII.

7   Joel Miller, *Lifted by Angels* (Thomas Nelson, Nashville, Tennessee, 2012), 63.

A good example of this is the account of Peter's deliverance from prison and death. Set to be executed the next day, he was jolted awake and led out of the prison by an angel. When he appeared at the door of the house where people were gathered to pray for him, they dismissed the report of his arrival as simply being the presence of his angel (Acts 12:1–17). Now frankly, if someone told me an angel was at the door, I'd go check it out. Not these folks! They kept on praying. They regarded angels as part of the normal rhythm of God's grace in their lives, and so should we.

As surely as an angel was sent to shut the mouths of the lions surrounding Daniel, so too may we expect God's angels to speed to our defense, guard us in our ways, and push back against the powers of darkness that assail us. That doesn't necessarily mean that we each have a particular angel assigned to us like George Bailey in *It's a Wonderful Life*. While that might be going beyond what the Scriptures say, it's well within the bounds of Scripture to note the power and presence of God's holy angels in our lives.

Each of the seven churches of Asia Minor appears to have had an "angel" assigned to it (Rev. 2–3), and Eden itself was guarded by fierce and armed cherubim (Gen. 3). While we look "through a glass darkly" (1 Cor. 13:12 KJV) at these mysteries, we can certainly rejoice that God's holy angels are present with us in worship (Rev. 4–5), minister to us (Heb. 1:14), and journey between the heavenly realm and our own through the mediating work of our Savior Jesus Christ (John 1:51; Gen. 28:12), the true ladder of Jacob that bridges the two realms to make them one.

DOES PAUL'S PHRASE "PRINCIPALITIES AND POWERS" REFER TO FALLEN ANGELS THAT ARE ASSIGNED TO RULE OVER CERTAIN NATIONS OR PEOPLE?

Paul uses this phrase in three key places in his letter to the Ephesians (1:20–21; 3:10–11; 6:12), as well as in Colossians (1:16; 2:14–15). New Testament scholar F.F. Bruce translated these "world forces" as "cosmocrats," spiritual rulers of various realms but all under the authority of Jesus Christ. What we note about them in these passages is, first, that they were created by and for Jesus; second, that he rules over them, indeed "high above" them; third, that they have fallen from their original station into disobedience to God and are violent opponents of the gospel and the church; fourth, that they have been defeated by Christ in his death on the cross and resurrection from the dead; and last, that through the church, God will show them his wisdom; that is, the cross of Christ that secures their demise.

These mysterious entities appear as part of a fallen angelic hierarchy of sorts, assigned to govern the earth but instead following the Dragon in his rebellion against God. Many early Christians believed in an angelic hierarchy but did not venture very far in how to best describe it, leaving that to later generations of church fathers. Some Jewish apocalyptic literature contained visions of these hierarchies. Daniel also mentions angelic "princes" assigned to various earthly kingdoms, notably Persia and Greece (Dan. 10). Daniel was engaged in fasting and prayer as angelic forces guarding his people were battling with these other "princes" until the arrival of Michael and Gabriel, two prominent powers associated with Israel and loyal to God. The cosmology that these Scriptures present was vital for Israel in their often terrible suffering under the hand of the despotic tyrannies of Babylon, Persia, Greece, and Rome. No matter how dark that world was, it was nonetheless under the hand of God who ruled all and would deliver them through the Son of Man when he came to establish the kingdom (Dan. 7:13–14)

Do such powers continue to rule over nations and peoples and regions of the globe? That's possibly the case, and I tend to believe that's likely the situation. But we must remember that these powers have authority only by permission of Christ the King and are dislodged from their thrones and dominions through the preaching of the gospel and the presence of the church as a visible witness to the Kingdom of God on earth. We don't need to try to discern what they are or where their sources of power may be. One early church was called to bear witness "where Satan's throne is" (Rev. 2:13). That's certainly a tough assignment! No matter what powers may be arrayed against the church in a certain place, Christ is Lord and will conquer them, doing so through the faithful, sacrificial witness of his people to the power of the cross.

RECOMMENDED RESOURCES

The Message of Ephesians: God's New Society, by John R.W. Stott
I Believe in Satan's Downfall, by Michael Green
Indwelling Sin in Believers, by John Owen
Lifted by Angels, by Joel Miller
Powers of Evil, by Sydney H.T. Page
Precious Remedies Against Satan's Devices, by Thomas Brooks
Talking Back, by Evagrius of Pontus
The Christian in Complete Armor, by William Gurnall
The Screwtape Letters, by C.S.Lewis
The Unseen Realm, by Michael S. Heiser
The Westminster Larger Catechism

FROM CORE RADIO:

» Can the devil read my mind? https://www.youtube.com/watch?v=m3Z3Y6QCOyg

» Can a Christian be possessed? https://www.youtube.com/watch?v=DIOdvHPZzu4

» Did God create the devil? (15:22) https://www.youtube.com/watch?v=DIOdvHPZzu4

» How do we respond to demonic activity? (21:27) https://corechristianity.com/resource-library/episodes/how-should-christians-respond-to-demon-possession/

» How does Satan work today? (5:30) https://www.youtube.com/watch?v=tFyDERIZkno

» Are aliens really just demons? https://www.youtube.com/watch?v=8LqQOGeXP3I&t=11s

» Who were the Nephilim? https://corechristianity.com/resource-library/episodes/who-were-the-nephilim/

» What are the signs of demon possession and what do we do about it when we see it? (11:05) https://corechristianity.com/resource-library/episodes/best-of-2019-what-are-the-signs-of-demon-possession/

FROM CORE CHRISTIANITY:

» Is Mental Illness Demonic Activity? https://corechristianity.com/resource-library/articles/mental-illness-and-demonic-activity/

» 10 Things You Should Know About Demons and Satan. https://corechristianity.com/resource-library/articles/10-things-you-should-know-about-demons-and-satan/

» Christians and Demonic Activity Today. https://corechristianity.com/resource-library/articles/christians-and-demonic-activity-today/

CAN THE DEVIL READ MY MIND?

More Booklets
Available

RESOURCES TO AID DISCIPLESHIP

Designed to help people find answers to common questions and dig deeper into foundational truths, our Core booklets are ideal tools for discipleship. Typically less than 100 pages, these concise booklets are written by trusted authors and provide rich, accessible content for personal reflection and group discussion.

- ✈ Tough Questions Answered
- ✈ Seeing Jesus: Four Portraits of an Unlikely Savior
- ✈ Why Would Anyone Get Married?
- ✈ Can the Devil Read My Mind?
- ✈ Called to War: The Christian and the Military
- ✈ What Is God's Will for Me?
- ✈ What Still Divides Us: The Difference between Protestants and Roman Catholics
- ✈ How to Keep Your Faith After High School

 CORECHRISTIANITY.COM/BOOKLETS

Made in the USA
Monee, IL
24 October 2023

45060245R00044